To
_____

From
_____

DOTUN OYEWOPO

50 Daily Faith Confessions

OYEWOPO

50 Daily Faith Confessions

PUBLISHED IN AUSTRALIA BY
ACHIEVERS WORLD

50 Daily Faith Confessions
Copyright © 2020 by Dotun Oyewopo.
All rights reserved.

Requests for information should be addressed to:
dotunoyewopo@gmail.com

This book, or parts thereof, may not be reproduced, stored in a retrieval system, or transmitted in any form or by any means, electronic, mechanical, photocopying, recording or otherwise, without the written permission of the publisher.

ISBN 978-0-6489792-1-0 (paperback)

Printed in Australia

Every attempt has been made to credit the sources of copyrighted material used in this book. If any such acknowledgment has been inadvertently omitted or miscredited, receipt of such information would be appreciated

Unless otherwise noted, all scriptures are from *The Holy Bible, New International Version*. Copyright © 1973, 1978, 1984, 2011 by Biblica, Inc.® Used by permission of Zondervan. All rights reserved worldwide. www.Zondervan.com.

Scripture quotations marked (KJV) are taken from the *King James Version of the Bible*.

Scripture quotations marked (NLT) are from the *Holy Bible, New Living Translation*. Copyright © 1996, 2004, 2007 by Tyndale House Foundation. Used by permission of Tyndale House Publishers Inc., Carol Stream, Illinois 60188. All rights reserved.

Scripture quotations marked (GW) are taken from GOD'S WORD® Copyright© 1995 by God's Word to the Nations. All rights reserved

Scripture quotations marked (MSG) are taken from *The Message*. Copyright © 1993, 1994, 1995, 1996, 2000, 2001, 2002 by Eugene H.Peterson.

Scripture quotations marked (GNT) are taken from the Holy Bible, Good News Translation. Copyright © 1992 by American Bible Society.

Scripture quotations marked (ISV) are taken from the Holy Bible, International Standard Version. Copyright © 1995–2014 by ISV Foundation. All rights reserved internationally. Used by permission of Davidson Press, LLC. S

Scripture quotations marked (ESV) are taken from the Holy Bible, English Standard Version, copyright © 2001 by Crossway Bibles, a division of Good News Publishers. Used by permission. All rights reserved.

Scripture quotations marked (CEV) are taken from Holy Bible: Contemporary English Version. Copyright © 1995 American Bible Society.

Scripture quotations marked (NAS) are taken from the New American Standard Bible , copyright © 1960, 1962, 1963, 1968, 1971, 1972, 1973, 1975, 1977, 1995 by the Lockman Foundation. Used by permission.

Scripture quotations marked (CSB) from the Holy Bible, The Christian Standard Bible. Copyright © 2017 by Holman Bible Publishers. Used by permission. All rights reserved.

Words and phrases in Scripture quotations that are in **bold** or *italics* are the emphasis of the author.

Dedication

This book is dedicated to those who are ready to ground the foundation of their life with faith confessions from their hearts.

This moment in your life is precious because God has destined that today, you will hold this book *50 Daily Faith Confessions*

I believe and I am convinced beyond any doubt that God wants you to ask boldly for His blessings over your life. God has promised to answer all our requests if we ask Him in prayer.

"In that day you will no longer ask me anything. Very truly I tell you, my Father will give you whatever you ask in my name. Until now you have not asked for anything in my name. Ask and you will receive, and your joy will be complete"

(John 16:23-24, NIV).

Acknowledgment

I acknowledge the maker of heaven and the earth, the almighty God, the inspirational giver, the giver of visions and dreams, the giver of wisdom, knowledge, and understanding.

You gave me the book title, as well as wisdom and knowledge through the Holy Spirit. I couldn't have done it without You.

To my dearest husband, Oluwafemi Emmanuel Oyekunle Oyewopo, thank you for always supporting me. You are my hero. I love you, my husband.

To my sons King David Boluwatife Abisoye Oyewopo and Father Abraham Adekolade Ayodeji Oyewopo, I am grateful to you both. I thank you for your encouragement and daily support. I am so proud to be called your mother.

REVIEW

A powerful book streamlined to show God's secret to success. With this daily confession one can begin to shape one's life into being a better version of self. The scriptures are appropriate to daily living and if used at the right time daily one can begin to enjoy a successful day.

Once done with the 50 days one is able to meditate on the word and continue to implement the 50 Days of confessing the faith.

May God continue to bless you with more revelation and power of His Word.

Connie Nxumalo

"The tongue has the power of life and death, and those who love it will eat its fruit"

— (Proverbs 8:21, NIV)

CONTENTS

Power of Confession 1
What to Do with Your Mouth 3
Power of Words 4
DAY 1 5
DAY 2 7
DAY 3 9
DAY 4 11
DAY 5 13
DAY 6 15
DAY 7 17
DAY 8 19
DAY 9 21
DAY 10 23
DAY 11 25
DAY 12 27
DAY 13 29
DAY 14 31
DAY 15 33
DAY 16 35
DAY 17 37
DAY 18 39

DAY 19	41
DAY 20	43
DAY 21	45
DAY 22	47
DAY 23	49
DAY 24	51
DAY 25	53
DAY 26	55
DAY 27	57
DAY 28	59
DAY 29	61
DAY 30	63
DAY 31	65
DAY 32	67
DAY 33	69
DAY 34	71
DAY 35	73
DAY 36	75
DAY 37	77
DAY 38	79
DAY 39	81
DAY 40	83
DAY 41	85

DAY 42	87
DAY 43	89
DAY 44	91
DAY 45	93
DAY 46	95
DAY 47	97
DAY 48	99
DAY 49	101
DAY 50	103
How to be saved	105

Power of Confession

Many believers do not understand confession—what it is and the power it has. Hence, we have not tapped into the full potential of our confessions. We have not seen or experienced the abundant promises of God in His Word.

Speaking the Word of God is completely different from confession. Therefore, it is important to understand the difference. Confession goes beyond simply speaking the Word. It is declaring what you are convinced of and hold to be true.

"The scripture says, 'I spoke because I believed.' In the same spirit of faith we also speak because we believe" (2 Corinthians 4:13, GNT).

With your heart you believe and with your mouth confession is made to righteousness. You must watch what you say because your confession either brings life or death. Our mouths are very powerful, so are the words that come out of them. The words we speak are alive and active.

"Watch your words and hold your tongue; you'll save yourself a lot of grief" (Proverbs 21:23, MSG).

"Words kill, words give life; they're either poison or fruit – you choose" (Proverbs 18:21, MSG).

"You are snared by the word of your mouth; you are taken by the words of your mouth"

(Proverbs 6:2, MSG).

"Let no corrupt communication proceed out of your mouth, but that which is good to the use of edifying, that it may minister grace unto the hearers" (Ephesians 4:29, KJV).

What to Do with Your Mouth

Your tongue is a very powerful God-given instrument. It can either call down blessings, grace, and abundance from heaven or bring curses, sickness, afflictions, and bondage (failure) into your life.

"Death and life are in the power of the tongue: **and** they that love it shall eat the fruit thereof" (Proverbs 18:21).

- Your mouth is a fountain of life; therefore, what comes out of it should be life.

"The mouth of the righteous is a fountain of life, but the mouth of the wicked conceals violence" (Proverbs 10:11, NIV).

- Think before you speak. Be slow to speak.

"My dear brothers and sisters, take note of this: Everyone should be quick to listen, slow to speak and slow to become angry" (James 1:19, NIV).

- Speak kind, encouraging words with your mouth that will bless people. Let the words you say benefit those who are listening to you.

"Do not let any unwholesome talk come out of your mouths, but only what is helpful for building others up according to their needs, that it may benefit those who listen" (Ephesians 4:29, NIV).

Power of Words

You have the power to make your words work for or against you. Whatever you say comes to pass. The Bible says when you decree a thing with your mouth, it is established in heaven. This is why you must speak words of life into yourself because you will surely eat the fruit.

Four Things Your Words Will Do to You

1. Your words can set you free or condemn you.

"For by your words you will be acquitted, and by your words you will be condemned" (Matthew 12:37).

2. **Your words can heal or make you sick.**

"Gracious words are a honeycomb, sweet to the soul and healing to the bones" (Proverbs 16:24, NIV).

"The mouths of fools are their undoing, and their lips are a snare to their very lives" (Proverbs 18:7, NIV).

3. **Your words can get you in or out of trouble.**

"Whoso keepeth his mouth and his tongue keepeth his soul from troubles" (Proverbs 21:23, NIV).

4. **Your words can give you life or death.**

"Death and life are in the power of the tongue, and those who love it will eat its fruit" (Proverbs 18:21, NKJV).

50 Daily Faith Confessions

DAY 1

Today, I confess that I am a product of God's Word. I am who God says I am.

"For we are God's masterpiece.
He has created us anew in Christ Jesus, so we can do the good things he planned for us long ago"

(Ephesians 2:10, NLT).

Scriptural Meditation

(Ephesians 2:10, NLT)

50 Daily Faith Confessions

DAY 2

Today, I confess that by the strength of God, I can do what the Word of God says I can do.

"I can do all things through Christ who strengthens me"

(Philippians 4:13, NKJV).

Scriptural Meditation

(Philippians 4:13, NKJV)

50 Daily Faith Confessions
DAY 3

Today, I confess that my destiny will not be wasted. I will live a meaningful life! A life of influence and affluence.

"The thief's purpose is to steal and kill and destroy. My purpose is to give them a rich and satisfying life"

(John 10:10, NLT).

Scriptural Meditation

(John 10:10, NLT)

50 Daily Faith Confessions

DAY 4

Today, I confess that I will succeed, break Barriers, and be fruitful in all I do.

"They are like trees that grow beside a stream, that bear fruit at the right time, and whose leaves do not dry up. They succeed in everything they do"

(Psalm 1:3, GNT).

Scriptural Meditation

(Psalm 1:3, GNT)

50 Daily Faith Confessions

DAY 5

Today, I confess that the favour of the almighty God will locate, surround, and shield me.

"You bless righteous people, O LORD. Like a large shield, you surround them with your favour"

(Psalm 5:12, GW).

Scriptural Meditation

(Psalm 5:12, GW)

50 Daily Faith Confessions
DAY 6

Today, I confess that
The love of God will locate me. The divine mercy of God will locate me.

"The steadfast love of the Lord never ceases; his mercies never come to an end; they are new every morning; great is your faithfulness"

(Lamentations 3:22-23, ESV).

Scriptural Meditation

(Lamentations 3:22-23, ESV)

50 Daily Faith Confessions

DAY 7

Today, I confess that city gates will open for me. Doors of divine opportunity will open for me, not one will stay closed.

"The LORD said to Cyrus, his chosen one: I have taken hold of your right hand to help you capture nations and remove kings from power. City gates will open for you; not one will stay closed"

(Isaiah 45:1, CEV).

Scriptural Meditation

(Isaiah 45:1, CEV)

50 Daily Faith Confessions

DAY 8

Today, I confess that My children will bring honour to me. I will not weep over them.

"May our sons flourish in their youth like well-nurtured plants. May our daughters be like graceful pillars, carved to beautify a palace"

(Psalm 144:12, NLT).

Scriptural Meditation

(Psalm 144:12, NLT)

50 Daily Faith Confessions
DAY 9

Today, I confess that I will be blessed in all I do. All my efforts will be crowned with good and fruitful success.

"The LORD will send rain at the proper time from his rich treasury in the heavens and will bless all the work you do. You will lend to many nations, but you will never need to borrow from them"

(Deuteronomy 28:12, NLT).

Scriptural Meditation

(Deuteronomy 28:12, NLT)

50 Daily Faith Confessions
DAY 10

Today, I confess that I will not build for others to inhabit. I will not labour in vain. I will enjoy the work of my hand.

"They won't build for others to inhabit; they won't plant for others to eat— for like the lifetime of a tree, so will the lifetime of my people be, and my chosen ones will long enjoy the work of their hands"

(Isaiah 65:22, ISV).

Scriptural Meditation

(Isaiah 65:22, ISV)

_____
_____
_____
_____
_____
_____
_____
_____
_____
_____
_____
_____
_____
_____
_____
_____
_____
_____
_____

50 Daily Faith Confessions

DAY 11

Today, I confess that
my God-given talents
will not be buried. They will manifest
for the world to see.

"Kings will be your foster fathers, and their queens your nursing mothers"

(Isaiah 49:23, NIV).

Scriptural Meditation

(Isaiah 49:23, NIV)

50 Daily Faith Confessions
DAY 12

Today, I confess that I will not eat the fruit of sorrow, tears, and bitterness.

"Then this Daniel distinguished himself above the governors and satraps, because an excellent spirit was in him; and the king gave thought to setting him over the whole realm"

(Daniel 6:3, NKJV).

Scriptural Meditation

(Daniel 6:3, NKJV)

50 Daily Faith Confessions
DAY 13

Today, I confess that I have received the spirit of boldness. I have a sound mind! I have the ability to reason and think.

"For God has not given us a spirit of fear, but of power and of love and of a sound mind"

(2 Timothy 1:7, NKJV).

Scriptural Meditation

(2 Timothy 1:7, NKJV)

50 Daily Faith Confessions
DAY 14

Today, I confess that I have understanding. I am productive and I have excellent wisdom.

"I have heard of you, that the Spirit of God is in you, and that light and understanding and excellent wisdom are found in you"

(Daniel 5:14, NKJV).

Scriptural Meditation

(Daniel 5:14, NKJV).

50 Daily Faith Confessions

DAY 15

Today, I confess that
by the help of the Holy Spirit, I will not do less than
God's purpose for my life.

"My nourishment comes from doing the will of God, who sent me, and from finishing his work"

(John 4:34, NLT).

Scriptural Meditation

(John 4:34, NLT)

50 Daily Faith Confessions
DAY 16

Today, I confess that
I will reign in life!
I receive abundant grace!
I am a champion!
I was born to win!

"For if by the one man's offense death reigned through the one, much more those who receive abundance of grace and of the gift of righteousness will REIGN IN LIFE through the One, Jesus Christ"

(Romans 5:17, NKJV).

Scriptural Meditation

(Romans 5:17, NKJV)

50 Daily Faith Confessions
DAY 17

Today, I confess that I am divinely empowered to do the supernatural.

"See, I will make you into a threshing sledge, new and sharp, with many teeth. You will thresh the mountains and crush them, and reduce the hills to chaff"

(Isaiah 41:15, NIV).

Scriptural Meditation

(Isaiah 41:15, NIV)

50 Daily Faith Confessions

DAY 18

Today, I confess that
I am standing up again.
I have no defects.
I am not a failure.

"No matter how often honest people fall, they always get up again"

(Proverbs 24:16, GNT).

Scriptural Meditation

(Proverbs 24:16, GNT)

Daily Faith Confessions
DAY 19

Today, I confess that I will never move downward. I am the head. I am made for the top.

"The LORD will make you the head and not the tail; you will only move upward and never downward"

(Deuteronomy 28:13, CSB).

Scriptural Meditation

(Deuteronomy 28:13, CSB)

50 Daily Faith Confessions

DAY 20

Today, I confess that my light is shining. God is bringing me to the limelight. God will send help to me.

"Arise, shine, for your light has come, and the glory of the Lord rises upon you. Nations will come to your light, and kings to the brightness of your dawn"

(Isaiah 60:1, 3).

"Strangers will stand and feed your flocks, and foreigners will be your plowmen and vinedressers"

(Isaiah 61:5).

Scriptural Meditation

(Isaiah 60:1, 3)

50 Daily Faith Confessions
DAY 21

Today, I confess that my face will not be covered in shame. My head is lifted high.

"I sought the Lord, and he answered me; he delivered me from all my fears. Those who look to him are radiant; their faces are never covered with shame"

(Psalm 34:4-5, NIV).

Scriptural Meditation

(Psalm 34:4-5, NIV)

50 Daily Faith Confessions

DAY 22

Today, I confess that the blessings of the God will be mine. The prosperity of God will be mine.

"You will eat the fruit of your labour; blessings and prosperity will be yours"

(Psalm 128:2, NIV).

Scriptural Meditation

(Psalm 128:2, NIV)

50 Daily Faith Confessions

DAY 23

Today, I confess that
I am secure on the Rock of Life. I am no more in the pit of life. The goodness of
God shall locate me.

"I waited patiently for the Lord's help; then he listened to me and heard my cry. He pulled me out of a dangerous pit, out of the deadly quicksand. He set me safely on a rock and made me secure"

(Psalm 40:1-3, GNT).

Scriptural Meditation

(Psalm 40:1-3, GNT)

50 Daily Faith Confessions
DAY 24

Today, I confess that I lack nothing in life. All my needs are divinely met.

"And my God shall supply all your needs according to His riches in glory by Christ Jesus"

(Philippians 4:19, NKJV).

Scriptural Meditation

(Philippians 4:19, NKJV)

50 Daily Faith Confessions
DAY 25

Today, I confess that my bread is blessed. My water is blessed. Sickness is taken away from me.

"So you shall serve the LORD your God, and He will bless your bread and your water. And I will take away sickness from among you"

(Exodus 23:25).

Scriptural Meditation

(Exodus 23:25)

50 Daily Faith Confessions

DAY 26

Today, I confess that I am covered by the feathers of God. I am protected under His wings. No harm shall locate me.

"He will cover you with his feathers, and under his wings you will find refuge... You will not fear the terror of night, nor the arrow that flies by day, nor the pestilence that stalks in the darkness, nor the plague that destroys at midday"

(Psalm 91:4-6, NIV).

Scriptural Meditation

(Psalm 91:4-6, NIV)

50 Daily Faith Confessions
DAY 27

Today, I confess that
I will not be put to shame.
I will not be disgraced.
I shall not be ridiculed.
I will not be humiliated.

"Do not be afraid; you will not be put to shame. Do not fear disgrace; you will not be humiliated. You will forget the shame of your youth and remember no more the reproach of your widowhood"

(Isaiah 54:4, NIV).

Scriptural Meditation

(Isaiah 54:4, NIV)

_____
_____
_____
_____
_____
_____
_____
_____
_____
_____
_____
_____
_____
_____
_____
_____
_____
_____
_____
_____

50 Daily Faith Confessions

DAY 28

Today, I confess that I have been shown the good path of life. I have fullness of joy. My joy shall know no bounds.

"You will show me the path of life; In Your presence is fullness of joy; At Your right hand are pleasures forevermore"

(Psalm 16:11, NKJV).

Scriptural Meditation

(Psalm 16:11, NKJV)

50 Daily Faith Confessions
DAY 29

Today, I confess that
I can do all things. I have
the strength of God.
My weakness has been exchanged
for the strength of the Lord.

"For I can do everything through Christ, who gives me strength"

(Philippians 4:13, NLT).

Scriptural Meditation

(Philippians 4:13, NLT)

50 Daily Faith Confessions
DAY 30

Today, I confess that my latter end will increase abundantly. I am delivered from smallness.

"For who has despised the day of small things?"

(Zechariah 4:10, NKJV).

"Though your beginning was small, yet your latter end would increase abundantly"

(Job 8:7, NKJV).

"Enlarge your house; build an addition. Spread out your home, and spare no expense! For you will soon be bursting at the seams. Your descendants will occupy other nations and resettle the ruined cities"

(Isaiah 54:2-3, NLT).

Scriptural Meditation

(Isaiah 54:2-3, NLT)

50 Daily Faith Confessions
DAY 31

Today, I confess that I have the mightiness of God. I am diligent.

"Whatever your hand finds to do, do it with your might; for there is no work or device or knowledge or wisdom in the grave where you are going"

(Ecclesiastes 9:10, NLV).

"And we desire that each one of you show the same diligence to the full assurance of hope until the end, that you do not become sluggish, but imitate those who through faith and patience inherit the promises"

(Hebrews 6:11-12, NKJV).

Scriptural Meditation

(Ecclesiastes 9:10, NLV)

50 Daily Faith Confessions

DAY 32

Today, I confess that the good Lord will comfort me on every side.

"Thou shalt increase my greatness, and comfort me on every side"

(Psalm 71:21, NKJV).

Scriptural Meditation

(Psalm 71:21, NKJV)

50 Daily Faith Confessions
DAY 33

Today, I confess that I receive the great plan of God for my life to prosper me.

"'For I know the plans I have for you,' declares the LORD, 'plans to prosper you and not to harm you, plans to give you hope and a future'"

(Jeremiah 29:11, NIV).

Scriptural Meditation

(Jeremiah 29:11, NIV)

50 Daily Faith Confessions
DAY 34

Today, I confess that I am changing. I will go from glory to higher glory in Christ.

"But we all, with open face beholding as in a glass the glory of the Lord, are changed into the same image from glory to glory, even as by the Spirit of the Lord"

(2 Corinthians 3:18, KJV).

Scriptural Meditation

(2 Corinthians 3:18, KJV).

50 Daily Faith Confessions
DAY 35

Today, I confess that
My path is shining brighter.

"But the path of the just *is* as the shining light, that shineth more and more unto the perfect day"

(Proverbs 4:18).

Scriptural Meditation

(Proverbs 4:18)

50 Daily Faith Confessions
DAY 36

Today, I confess that I am blessed of the Lord. I am surrounded with favour.

"Surely, LORD, you bless the righteous; you surround them with your favor as with a shield"

(Psalm 5:12, NIV).

Scriptural Meditation

(Psalm 5:12, NIV)

50 Daily Faith Confessions
DAY 37

Today, I confess that I will overcome. The peace of God is with me.

"These things I have spoken unto you, that in me ye might have peace. In the world ye shall have tribulation: but be of good cheer; I have overcome the world"

(John 16:33, KJV).

Scriptural Meditation

(John 16:33, KJV)

50 Daily Faith Confessions

DAY 38

Today, I confess that I am set free from worries. My hope is in God.

"Why, my soul, are you downcast? Why so disturbed within me? Put your hope in God, for I will yet praise him, my Savior and my God"

(Psalm 42:11, NIV).

Scriptural Meditation

(Psalm 42:11, NIV)

50 Daily Faith Confessions

DAY 39

Today, I confess that I am valuable to God. I am set free from worries.

"Therefore I tell you, do not worry about your life, what you will eat or drink; or about your body, what you will wear. Is not life more than food, and the body more than clothes? Look at the birds of the air; they do not sow or reap or store away in barns, and yet your heavenly Father feeds them. Are you not much more valuable than they? Can any one of you by worrying add a single hour to your life?"

(Matthew 6:25-27, NIV).

Scriptural Meditation

(Matthew 6:25-27, NIV)

50 Daily Faith Confessions
DAY 40

Today, I confess I have a future that is planned by God.

"For I know the plans I have for you, declares the Lord, plans for welfare and not for evil, to give you a future and a hope"

(Jeremiah 29:11, ESV).

Scriptural Meditation

(Jeremiah 29:11, ESV)

50 Daily Faith Confessions

DAY 41

Today, I confess that I am endowed with divine honour.

"Blessed is the one who finds wisdom, and the one who gets understanding, for the gain from her is better than gain from silver and her profit better than gold. She is more precious than jewels, and nothing you desire can compare with her. Long life is in her right hand; in her left hand are riches and honor. Her ways are ways of pleasantness, and all her paths are peace"

(Proverbs 3:13-18, ESV).

Scriptural Meditation

(Proverbs 3:13-18, ESV)

50 Daily Faith Confessions
DAY 42

Today, I confess that I have heavenly Understanding and wisdom.

"For the Lord gives wisdom; from his mouth come knowledge and understanding"

(Proverbs 2:6, NIV).

Scriptural Meditation

(Proverbs 2:6, NIV)

50 Daily Faith Confessions
DAY 43

Today, I confess that I am endowed with divine abilities. I am endowed with divine knowledge.

"The Spirit of the LORD will rest on him— the Spirit of wisdom and of understanding, the Spirit of counsel and of might, the Spirit of the knowledge and fear of the LORD"

(Isaiah 11:2, NIV).

Scriptural Meditation

(Isaiah 11:2, NIV)

50 Daily Faith Confessions
DAY 44

Today, I confess that I have sufficiency in all I do. God is able to make all grace abound for me.

"And God is able to make all grace abound to you, so that having all sufficiency in all things at all times, you may abound in every good work"

(2 Corinthians 9:8, ESV).

Scriptural Meditation

(2 Corinthians 9:8, ESV)

50 Daily Faith Confessions

DAY 45

Today, I confess that I am God's handiwork. I am created to do good works.

"For we are God's handiwork, created in Christ Jesus to do good works, which God prepared in advance for us to do"

(Ephesians 2:10, NIV).

Scriptural Meditation

(Ephesians 2:10, NIV)

50 Daily Faith Confessions
DAY 46

Today, I confess that the days of my mourning are over. God is my everlasting light.

"Thy sun shall no more go down, neither shall thy moon withdraw itself; for Jehovah will be thine everlasting light, and the days of thy mourning shall be ended"

(Isaiah 60:20, ASV).

Scriptural Meditation

(Isaiah 60:20, ASV)

50 Daily Faith Confessions
DAY 47

Today, I confess that
I will arise and shine. The glory of God is risen
upon me. I will reign.

"Arise, shine; for your light has come, and the glory of the LORD has risen upon you"

(Isaiah 60:1, NAS).

Scriptural Meditation

(Isaiah 60:1, NAS)

50 Daily Faith Confessions
DAY 48

Today, I confess that I will not sorrow. I will not cry. I shall not mourn.

"And God shall wipe away all tears from their eyes; and there shall be no more death, neither sorrow, nor crying, neither shall there be any more pain: for the former things are passed away"

(Revelation 21:4, KJV).

Scriptural Meditation

(Revelation 21:4, KJV)

50 Daily Faith Confessions
DAY 49

Today, I confess that I am born to subdue the earth. I am born to reign, and I am fruitful.

"God blessed them and said to them, "Be fruitful and increase in number; fill the earth and subdue it. Rule over the fish in the sea and the birds in the sky and over every living creature that moves on the ground"

(Genesis 1:28, NIV).

Scriptural Meditation

(Genesis 1:28, NIV)

50 Daily Faith Confessions
DAY 50

Today, I confess that I am coming out of shame, reproach, and disgrace to honour and praise!

"Do not be afraid, for you will not be put to shame; do not be humiliated, for you will not be disgraced. For you will forget the shame of your youth and remember no more the reproach of your widowhood"

(Isaiah 54:4).

Scriptural Meditation

(Isaiah 54:4)

How to be saved

If you don't know God personally, here are four principles that will help guide you into a relationship with Him:

1. GOD LOVES YOU AND CREATED YOU TO KNOW HIM PERSONALLY

The most well-known verse in the Bible says, *"God so loved the world, that he gave his only Son, that whoever believes in him should not perish but have eternal life"* (John 3:16, ESV).

You see, this life is not the end of us. This life is preparation for eternity. We have the freedom to decide where we want to spend eternity: with God or apart from Him.

God thinks you're so valuable He wants to spend eternity with you! The Bible says, *"Now this is eternal life: that they may know you, the only true God, and Jesus Christ, whom you have sent"* (John 17:3).

He planned the universe and orchestrated history, including the details of our lives, so that we could become His friends.

So what prevents us from knowing God personally?

2. MAN IS SINFUL AND SEPARATED FROM GOD, SO WE CANNOT KNOW HIM PERSONALLY OR EXPERIENCE HIS LOVE BECAUSE OF OUR SINS

The Bible says, *"All have sinned and fall short of the glory of God"* (Romans 3:23).

Visualize God in heaven and man on the earth with a great gulf separating the two. Man is continually trying to reach God and establish a personal relationship with Him through His own efforts such as a good life, philosophy, or religion—but he inevitably fails.

The Bible says, "*The wages of sin is death* [separation from God]" (Romans 6:23). The third principle explains the only way to bridge this separation.

3. JESUS CHRIST IS GOD'S ONLY PROVISION FOR MAN'S SIN. THROUGH HIM ALONE CAN WE KNOW GOD PERSONALLY AND EXPERIENCE GOD'S LOVE

JESUS DIED IN OUR PLACE

"*God demonstrates his own love for us in this: While we were still sinners, Christ died for us*" (Romans 5:8, NIV).

HE ROSE FROM THE DEAD

"*Christ died for our sins, just as the Scriptures said. He was buried, and he was raised from the dead on the third day, just as the Scriptures said. He was seen by Peter and then by the Twelve. After that, he was seen by more than 500 of his followers at one time*" (1 Corinthians 15:3-6, NLT).

HE IS THE ONLY WAY TO GOD

"*Jesus said to him, 'I am the way, and the truth, and the life; no one comes to the Father, but through Me'*" (John 14:6, NASB).

Visualize now that God has bridged the gulf that separates us from Him by sending His Son, Jesus Christ, to die on the cross in our place to pay the penalty for our sins. Yet, it's not enough just to know these truths.

4. WE MUST INDIVIDUALLY RECEIVE JESUS CHRIST AS SAVIOR AND LORD; THEN WE CAN KNOW GOD PERSONALLY AND EXPERIENCE HIS LOVE

WE MUST RECEIVE CHRIST

"As many as received him, to them he gave the right to become children of God, even to those who believe in his name" (John 1:12, NASB).

WE RECEIVE CHRIST THROUGH FAITH

"It is by grace you have been saved, through faith-and this not from yourselves, it is the gift of God-not by works, so that no one can boast" (Ephesians 2:8–9, NIV).

WHEN WE RECEIVE CHRIST, WE EXPERIENCE A NEW BIRTH

The Bible tells of how a man named Nicodemus experienced a new birth through Christ:

There was a man named Nicodemus, a Jewish religious leader who was a Pharisee. After dark one evening, he came to speak with Jesus. "Rabbi," he said, "we all know that God has sent you to teach us. Your miraculous signs are evidence that God is with you." Jesus replied, "I tell you the truth, unless you are born again, you cannot see the Kingdom of God." "What do you mean?" exclaimed Nicodemus. "How can an old man go back into his mother's womb and be born again?" Jesus replied, "I assure you, no one can enter the Kingdom of God without being born of water and the Spirit. Humans can reproduce only human life, but the Holy Spirit gives birth to spiritual life. So don't be surprised when I say, You must be born again. The wind blows wherever it wants. Just as you can hear the wind but can't tell where it comes from or where it is going, so you can't explain how people are born of the Spirit (John 3:1-8, NLT)

WE RECEIVE CHRIST BY PERSONAL INVITATION

Jesus Christ says, *"Behold, I stand at the door and knock; if anyone hears my voice and opens the door, I will come in to him and dine with him, and he with me"* (Revelation 3:20, NASB).

Receiving Christ involves turning to God from self and trusting Christ to come into our lives to forgive us of our sins and to make us what He wants us to be. Just to agree intellectually that Jesus Christ is the Son of God and that He died on the cross for our sins is not enough. Nor is it enough to have an emotional experience. We receive Jesus Christ by faith as an act of our free will.

HOW YOU CAN RECEIVE CHRIST RIGHT NOW BY FAITH THROUGH PRAYER

Prayer is just talking with God. He knows your heart, so don't worry about getting your words just right. Here is a suggested prayer to guide you:

Lord Jesus, I want to know You personally. Thank You for dying on the cross for my sins.

I open the door of my life and receive You as my Saviour and Lord. Thank You for forgiving me of my sins and giving me eternal life. Take control of my life. Make me the kind of person You want me to be.

Does this prayer express the desire of your heart? If it does, pray this prayer right now, and Christ will come into your life as promised.

Did you pray to receive Christ just now?

If so, congratulations! Luke 15:7 says that when one sinner accepts Jesus Christ as his or her Saviour, the angels rejoice. So there's a party going on in heaven right now over your decision! Remember this date as your "second birthday," the day you were born into a new life in Christ! You have God's Word that He answered your prayer.

The Bible promises eternal life to all who receive Christ: *"God has given us eternal life, and this life is in his Son. He who has the Son has the life; he who does not have the Son of God does not have the life. I write these things to you who believe in the name of the Son of God so that you may know that you have eternal life"* (1 John 5:11–13, NIV).

Thank God often that Christ is in your life, and He will never leave you (Hebrews 13:5).

You can know on the basis of His promise that Christ lives in you, and you have eternal life from the very moment you invited Him in.

Other books by Dotun Oyewopo

As glorious women, our self-worth should be based on the light of the knowledge God has shone into our hearts through His Word. The Word of God has clearly defined who we are and who we are not, what we are and what we are not.

Many women focus on their outward adornment; they are very concerned about how they look on the outside because that's what people can see.

However, the Bible clearly states that your physical beauty is not the most important aspect of who you are. A lot of women place greater value on clothes, shoes, bags, cars, and jewellery than on the Holy Spirit inside them. Of course, it is easy to boast about the trappings and riches we have, but that is not what God sees as most significant when He looks at us.

The book *The Glorious Woman* is the secret to manifesting the beautiful woman in you and helps you to know how you can influence your home, marriage, family, children, career, and ministry positively.

The Bible verses and prayer points are to build, guide, and keep you focused.

Arise and shine daughter of God, for the glory of the Lord is risen upon you.

50 Daily Faith Confessions for My Son

Speak life into your son with these powerful daily confessions. What you say will boost his present and future. Do you want your son to reach his full potential? Do you wish him a life of good health, great relationships, and prosperity? Do you want him to live godly and reflect the character of God?

Boldly declare these confessions daily and invoke God's blessings on your son. Then watch the remarkable transformation. *Fifty Daily Faith Confessions for My Son* is an impactful prayer guide filled with original declarations and Scripture-based prayer points. It is grounded in the Word and helps you to focus on making specific, strategic proclamations.

In this ungodly world, our sons are struggling to live with purpose and purity and to find their identity. Condemnation, shame, guilt, lack of ambition, rebellion, and fear are haunting many lives. But you can help your son live to conquer. Make these declarations and help him overcome life's obstacles. He will become the man God wants him to be. Using these confessions is a great way to pray for your son no matter his age. Whether a toddler, teen, or adult, your words will be life-changing and potent. As you speak them, you will both experience the abundant promises of God in His Word.

You possess what you confess!

50 Daily Faith Confessions for Your Daughter

Speak life into your daughters with these powerful daily confessions. What you say will make the difference now and in the future. Do you want your daughter to reach her full potential? Do you wish her a life of good health, great relationships, and prosperity? Do you want her to live godly and manifest all the promises of God?

Boldly declare these confessions daily and invoke God's blessings on your daughter. Then watch the remarkable transformation. *Fifty Daily Faith Confessions for My Daughter* is an impactful prayer guide filled with original declarations and Scripture-based prayer points. It is grounded in the Word and helps you to focus on making specific, strategic proclamations.

The world can be a harsh place for girls and women to live. Evil pronouncements—heard and unheard—are made every day over them, some even before birth. This book is a critical tool for every mother and father to break generational and other curses on your daughter's life. Get a copy today and reverse the curses of death, rebellion, low self-esteem, barrenness, failed marriages, negative self-talk, and other ills. As you do so, you will both experience the abundant promises of God in His Word.

You possess what you confess!

www.ingramcontent.com/pod-product-compliance
Lightning Source LLC
Chambersburg PA
CBHW020326010526
44107CB00054B/1997